Maldives Travel Guide 2023

The ultimate travel guide to Maldives: Discover what to see, where to stay in the Tropical island of Maldives with well planned itinerary guide for first timers

Steven S. Bender

All right reserved. No part of this publication may be reduced,
distributed, or transmitted in any form or by any means,
including photocopying, recording, or any other electronic or
or mechanical methods, without the prior written permission
of the publisher, except in the case of brief quotations embodied
in critical reviews and certain other non-commercial uses
permitted by copyright law.
Copyright @Steven S.Bender ,2023

Table Of Content

Introduction
WHY GO TO MALDIVES
TOP 5 THINGS TO SEE AND DO IN MALDIVES
OTHER THINGS TO SEE AND DO IN MALDIVES
MALDIVES TRAVEL COST
BACKPACKING THE MALDIVES SUGGESTED BUDGETS
MONEY SAVING TIPS
HOW TO GET AROUND MALDIVES
WHEN TO GO TO MALDIVES
HOW TO STAY SAFE IN MALDIVES
WHAT YOU NEED TO KNOW
CULTURE & CUSTOMS
WHAT TO EAT
MALDIVES VISA

DOS AND DON'TS IN THE MALDIVES
MALDIVES 10 DAYS ITINERARY GUIDE
TOP BEST HOTELS IN MALDIVES

12 TOP BEACHES IN MALDIVES THAT YOU MUST VISIT
CONCLUSION

Introduction

The Maldives is one of the most sought-after luxury destinations in the world, evoking visions of luxurious resorts and jet-set couples relaxing in beachside villas and swimming in turquoise seas. Although the Maldives is home to all of those things and is recognized as a premium location for spending out, it's still feasible to vacation here without fully breaking the bank.

Situated in the Indian Ocean, this secluded nation of 1,192 islands and 26 coral atolls is brimming with world-class diving and snorkeling. There are a wealth of possibilities to wander beyond the hotel resort bubble and soak in the magnificent remoteness of this tropical paradise.

Due to a considerably better boat transportation infrastructure and the setting up of independent guesthouses, the Maldives is growing into a (little more) budget-friendly holiday place.

This travel guide to the Maldives may help you plan your vacation, save money, and make the most of your stay in this stunning tropical retreat!

WHY GO TO MALDIVES

You've seen photographs of the Maldives before: picture-perfect private homes hanging above startling blue seas, pristine white sand beaches, and magnificent sunsets lowering towards the horizon. The breathtaking magnificence of the Maldives is something to witness, something you can't truly appreciate unless you're there in person.

The island country of the Maldives is popular with honeymooners wanting privacy and adventurers eager to explore the depths of the sea on a scuba diving and snorkeling expedition.

Visitors seeking leisure may reside at one of the island spas and all tourists should undoubtedly spend a day seeing the Maldives capital of Malé. The hotels in this area are likewise stunning, ranging from underwater hotels to overwater bungalows to magnificent resorts. Nevertheless, getting to and living in this tropical paradise demands patience (there are no direct flights from the United States) and enough cash. Situated between the Arabian and Laccadive seas, some 500 miles southwest of Sri Lanka, the Maldives is about as secluded as you can get - and that's just another one of its numerous allures.

TOP 5 THINGS TO SEE AND DO IN MALDIVES

1. Discover Malé

The Maldives' capital, albeit tiny, offers lots of things to see and do. Seet the nation's 17th-century mosque (Hukuru Miskiiy) and receive a historical overview of the country at the National Museum. Make sure to get a coffee and watch the world go by at one of the pleasantly chaotic cafés too.

2. Go diving

The Maldives is one of the top diving locations in the world. Observe hammerheads at Rasdhoo Madivaru (aka Hammerhead Point) or free dive with whale sharks. There are also many mantas and marine turtles here. Single-tank dives start at 775 MVR.

3. Relax on the beach

Outside the private resorts, Omadoo (on the South Ari Atoll) and Ukulhas Island (on the Alif Alif Atoll) are two of the nicest beaches in the nation. Manadhoo is another excellent site also. But make sure you're on a designated 'Bikini Beach' (a beach particularly for westerners) (a beach specifically for westerners).

4. Savor the food

The fish here is beyond excellent and extremely fresh. Most of the restaurants in Malé feature outdoor eating spaces. Some of the more popular locations to go to are The Seagull Café, Symphony, Royal Garden Café, and Irudhashu Hotaa (for fast meals) (for quick meals).

5. Try some watersports

Banana boats (inflatable boats pushed behind a speedboat), parasailing, water skiing, jet skiing, snorkeling, and kayaking may all be found here. Costs vary from 380 MVR for snorkeling to 2,000 MVR per person for tandem parasailing.

OTHER THINGS TO SEE AND DO IN MALDIVES

1. Treat yourself to a spa day

Even when you're on a small budget, it's nice to indulge in an additional dose of R&R. Anticipate spending at least 1,000 MVR for a 30-minute massage. Some of the bigger hotels offer discounts for early-morning/late-evening reservations so check with your hotel, Airbnb host, or guesthouse to find out about bargains.

2. Go fishing

Seafood is a vital aspect of Maldives cuisine. Most hotels and guesthouses hire poles, and bait, and give a guide for approximately 775 MVR. Skipjack and yellowfin tuna, wahoo, mahi-mahi, bigeye scad, and mackerel scad are all often found here. If you're an experienced fisherman, some of the greatest game fishing in the world can be done here. Expect to spend at least 3,000 MVR for a half-day shared charter.

3. Snorkel on the Baa Atoll

The Baa Atoll is a 1,200-square-kilometer (463-square-mile) UNESCO Biosphere Reserve overflowing with manta rays and whale sharks. On a clear day, you can see them swarming below the surface. It's just a five-minute boat journey from Dharavandhoo Island but accessing the region is highly restricted and there is an 80-person capacity so as not to harm the unique ecology. The entrance is roughly 550 MVR, which allows you 45 minutes in the water and a qualified snorkel guide. Proceeds go towards the Baa Atoll Conservation Fund.

4. Visit the National Art Museum

Founded in 1999, there's no permanent gallery here so make careful to check the website in advance since the space is left vacant if there is no visiting exhibition on show. The temporary shows at the gallery, which vary from traditional paintings and local textiles to worldwide contemporary artists, are worth a visit.

5. Dive the Maldive Victory

In 1981, this 100-meter-long (328-foot) cargo ship struck a shoal and sank. It's currently an amazing diving destination for experienced divers. Lying between 15-31 meters (50-100 feet) below the surface, there are powerful currents here that keep the tropical fish moving through the wreckage — but they also make it a tough dive location. There are many sorts of coral, fish, and sponges here. It's accessible all year round.

6. Visit the Malé Seafood Market

Come here and get a peek at Maldivians carrying out their everyday routine in the commercial core of Malé. Pick a fish (if you can muster your way through a purchase since most fishermen don't understand English) and have it grilled at your accommodation for supper.

7. Wash up on a sandbank

These little mounds of sand amid the Indian Ocean are the closest you can come to feeling like you're on your private island. Individual visits may be organized to any one of the hundred various banks located across the islands (many of which are related to/affiliated with resorts). Trips normally take 2-3 hours and cost 900 MVR.

8. Skip Maafushi

Maafushi, formerly a tranquil small island, is now the victim of unrestrained development. Hotels are popping erected left and right, boats making regular excursions to Malé to pick up tour groups, and an increasingly-crowded and overbuilt beach. The few eateries on the island cater largely to tourists and beyond the area cleaned up for visitors, it's one trash-covered mess. Skip it!

9. Perform all the watersports

Diving and snorkeling to observe the creatures beneath the ocean are what the Maldives is renowned for but there's much more to do. Most resorts provide kayaks, paddleboards, and paddle boats that you may use for free. Others provide surfing, windsurfing, and kitesurfing programs for both beginners and expert surfers (May October is the optimum period for this)

(May-October is the best time for this). Then you've got things like banana boating, tubing, jet skiing, sailing, parasailing, and flyboarding which are all also commonly accessible.

10. Stay on a local island

Most people stay in the high-end resorts when they travel to the Maldives but there's so much more to the islands than this. Local islands provide you the opportunity to get to know the Maldives as a nation rather than simply seeing a resort and a ton of biodiverse marine life. The nearby islands are where you may get cheaper guesthouse lodging, and there is more choice in terms of tour operators, restaurants, and other things to do. Fulidhoo, Ukulhas, Rasdhoo, and Thinadhoo were some of the most popular selections. Generally speaking, the farther out from the city you come the more laid-back and calm the islands are.

MALDIVES TRAVEL COST

Accommodation - Private rooms at guesthouses are likely to be your cheapest choice in the Maldives, with costs beginning from 625 MVR per night.

Resorts start at 6,000 MVR per night (not counting the private speed boats or seaplane transportation you need to reach there) (not including the private speed boats or seaplane transfers you need to arrive there). These may cost upwards of 30,000 MVR a night, making this a perfect spot to utilize whatever hotel points you have stored up.

Airbnb is accessible across the islands with private rooms beginning at 700 MVR, while 1,200 MVR is more frequent. For a complete home/apartment, rates start at 1,500 MVR but may go as high as 6,000 MVR or more! Whole homes/apartments are significantly less frequent so make sure to reserve in advance if you want one.

Wild camping isn't feasible since all land surrounding the islands is owned. The only genuine camping option is to ask to pitch a tent in someone's backyard, however, this isn't a guaranteed solution so forgo camping here.

Cuisine - Traditional food in the Maldives is focused on fish, coconuts, and rice. Tubers like taro and sweet potatoes are also frequent mainstays. Apart from various types of fish and seafood soups and stews, make sure to taste favorites such as gula (fried fish packed dough balls), kuli (spicy fish cakes), and dessert delicacies like bondi bai (Maldivian rice pudding) (Maldivian rice pudding).

Most typical dinners cost less than 70 MVR at informal local eateries while most resorts and hotels provide meals as restaurants here are sparse.

For a three-course lunch of traditional cuisine at a budget-friendly hotel, expect to spend roughly 300 MVR with a drink.

Alcohol is normally restricted but may be found at most luxury resorts. Prepare to pay a premium for it: beer costs upwards of 125 MVR while cocktails are twice that. A latte or cappuccino costs 35 MVR whereas a bottle of water is 5 MVR.

If you're planning to prepare your meals, make sure you stock up at the STO trade center in Malé. Buying here might save you a little additional money, particularly if you are staying someplace with a kitchen. Pricing here is frequently more competitive than street sellers and there is a fantastic choice of fresh fruits, vegetables, and other daily staples.

For a week's worth of necessities like rice, fruit, and fish, expect to spend roughly 700 MVR.

Activities — Single-tank dives start at 775 MVR while watersports (snorkeling, parasailing, water skiing, jet-skiing, snorkeling, and kayaking) start at 380 MVR and go up to 2,000 MVR per person for things like tandem parasailing. Spa treatments start at 1,000 MVR while fishing trips cost 3,000 MVR.

BACKPACKING MALDIVES SUGGESTED BUDGETS

If you are backpacking the Maldives, my advised budget is 1,100 MVR per day. This implies you're living at a budget guesthouse, preparing all of your meals, not drinking alcohol, riding public ferries to go about (but generally sticking to one island), and enjoying free and inexpensive activities like snorkeling and resting at the beach.

With a mid-range budget of 4,300 MVR, you can stay in a cheap hotel or private Airbnb, dine out for most of your meals, take some guided tours, go diving, do some water sports, visit a few islands, and use the odd private water taxi to move about.

On a "luxury" budget of 9,500 MVR or more per day, you may stay in a hotel, drink alcohol, dine out for all your meals, island-hop, and enjoy additional activities and guided excursions such as fishing charters and parasailing. This is simply the lowest level for luxury, however. The sky's the limit!

MONEY SAVING TIPS

The Maldives is a tough area to save money hence non-resort tourism is quite new to the nation. There are just a few things you can do to minimize your budget here:

Carry lots of cash - Despite the Maldives having its currency (MVR), US dollars are generally accepted — and you typically receive a better bargain if you pay in USD. This varies from one restaurant or business to another, so carry both and pay whichever provides you with the greatest rate. There are just ATMs in Malé.

Carry a reusable water bottle - The tap water here is not safe to drink so make sure you bring a reusable bottle with you. To keep safe, pack a water filter like LifeStraw to guarantee your water is pure and free from germs. It saves you money and preserves the environment too!

Island hop via ferry - The Maldives' islands are serviced by a succession of boats from Malé. They run on opposite days (to Maafushi on Monday, returning to Malé on Tuesday) and seldom on Friday (the Muslim sabbath) (the Muslim sabbath). You may hop from Malé to an atoll's major island and then to smaller, adjacent islands in the chain. Ferries cost between 55-150 MVR depending on the distance. Plan and research the ferries beforehand so you can avoid paying for a private speedboat.

Contemplate all-inclusive packages — The taxes and import levies on food and drink mean that you don't have many eateries to select from. Some hotels offer amazing discounts which include meals, beverages, and even premium services such as watersports, complimentary yoga lessons, or spa treatments.

Employ a travel agency for resort stays — This may seem paradoxical for a budget traveler but brokers that specialize in

Maldives tourism frequently have access to better prices than you can discover on the internet. These rates often include speedboat or seaplane transfer charges and you may even discover that you obtain upgrades on arrival .

Book in advance - Although most budget travelers work out their arrangements on arrival, planning offers numerous perks. For starters, Airbnbs, guesthouses, and hotels might become full up in busy seasons so your alternatives may be restricted. If you have booked in advance, your hotel or friendly villa/guesthouse owner may assist simplify transportation and organizing activities.

HOW TO GET AROUND MALDIVES

Boat — The unreliable but reasonably-priced public boat is a no-brainer for independent travelers, with ferries beginning at 55 MVR depending on the route. If you're going to visit an island further out from Malé, you need to do some island hopping using the boat system. This could need you to stay overnight on an island along the route since the boats do not operate every day or frequently. Most ferries also do not operate on the weekends.

Several of the islands farther out can only be accessible by private boat or aircraft. Verify the boat timetable well in advance and prepare appropriately (I didn't and it threw off my entire agenda).

Private speed boats cost from 385-1,500 MVR per person depending on the distance from Malé.

Air - Flying is exceedingly costly here. Flights from Malé to the neighboring islands cost up to 7,000 MVR each trip. Avoid flying if you want to keep on a budget!

WHEN TO GO TO MALDIVES

The Maldives is a year-round vacation with temperatures ranging between 23-31°C (74-89°F). The peak season spans from December to April, when flight and accommodation costs climb considerably (particularly around Christmas, New Year, Chinese New Year, and Easter) (especially around Christmas, New Year, Chinese New Year, and Easter). Book in advance if you plan to come during this time.

Don't be too worried about booking during the monsoon time, which spans from May to October. You may enjoy fewer people, better prices, and lots of bright days in between the few-and-far wet periods.

Diving is great throughout the year. For other activities, including surfing, the finest breaks are from mid-February through November.

HOW TO STAY SAFE IN MALDIVES

The Maldives is an exceedingly safe place for travelers. Keep a check on your things in public locations in Malé, which is more prone to petty crime (but at a very low level) (although at a very low level). On the other islands, particularly the resort-focused ones, it's exceedingly, incredibly unlikely anything is going to happen to you or your things. So, it's usually a good idea to avoid leaving any valuables on the beach while you swim.

Single female visitors should feel secure here, however, the typical precautions apply (always keep an eye on your drink while out, never go home alone at night, etc) (always keep an eye on your drink when out, never walk home alone at night, etc.)

Except for the 2004 tsunami, large-scale natural catastrophes are uncommon.

Nonetheless, climate change has contributed to an escalation in greater rainfall, storm surges, and small coastal floods. Be sure you have travel insurance when you visit.

Observe the Muslim norms by sticking to clothing rules, particularly in the capital, where resort attire isn't usual. Do not consume alcohol outside your resort since penalties are likely.

Although scams here are uncommon, you may learn about typical travel scams to avoid here if you're concerned about being ripped off.

If you have an emergency, phone 119 for help.

Always believe your gut sense. Make copies of your papers, including your passport and ID. Send your itinerary along to loved ones so they'll know where you are.

The most crucial piece of advice I can provide is to obtain adequate travel insurance. Travel insurance protects you against sickness, accidents, theft, and cancellations. It's full protection in case anything goes wrong. I never go on a vacation without it since I've had to use it several times in the past. You may use the widget below to discover the insurance suited for you.

WHAT YOU NEED TO KNOW

Tap water is desalinated
This purified water is acceptable for bathing and brushing teeth, but you'll likely want to consume bottled water in the Maldives. Of note, bottled water may be rather pricey at resorts, so consider filling up with a few bottles at a local shop in Malé before traveling to your accommodation.

It's hot
These islands are situated near the equator, so the temperatures are pleasant year-round and the sun is powerful. Be sure to use a generous quantity of sunscreen to protect your skin from the sun's UV radiation.

The Islamic tradition is essential
The Maldives is a strict Muslim country, where you'll find lots of mosques and relatively little alcohol outside the resorts' boundaries.

CULTURE & CUSTOMS

The Maldives has been an Islamic country since the 12th century. With this rich background, you'll discover religious traditions embedded in the culture. Mosques dot the city of Malé, and you'll notice some men and women dressed in fairly modest garb. Should you choose to attend a mosque, you too should dress similarly; however, be aware that certain mosques are restricted to non-Muslims.

You'll also observe folks praying in public at particular times throughout the day. Be courteous by dropping your voice and avoid stepping in front of individuals who are praying. Most of these obvious cultural and religious traditions have been taken from the resorts. Yet, especially during Ramadan, expect to encounter certain Islamic rituals, such as local eateries shutting for the midday when the populace would be fasting.

Public demonstrations of love, such as kissing or hand-holding, are forbidden. Alcohol is banned, too, however, it is accessible and may be drunk on resort islands. Homosexuality is likewise outlawed in this island country. Men and women should be dressed modestly while going to and from the airport, and throughout Male' and Hulhumale'.

With hundreds of resort islands, the Maldives rely on tourism as its primary economy which pulls on a substantial share of the workforce. The second main business is fishing, and the tiny island country sells its marine catches to nations around the globe. The Maldives' currency is the rufiyaa and $1 equals roughly 15 rufiyaas. Nevertheless, the currency rate might vary so be careful to verify it before you fly.

The official language of the Maldives is Dhivehi yet many Maldivians speak and comprehend English, particularly those working at high-end resorts.

WHAT TO EAT

Food in the Maldives depends significantly on the region's accessible resources, which means fish, coconut, and starches figure strongly in many meals. Tuna, wahoo, and mahi mahi are a few of the seafood you may expect to see on menus in the Maldives. Other popular foods in the Maldives include samosas (pastries packed with savory stuffing such as spiced potatoes and veggies), curries, and spicy fried seafood.

Keep in mind, since the Maldives is an Islamic country, the majority does not consume alcohol. Yet, you will be allowed to drink alcoholic beverages at most establishments.

If you're staying at a high-end resort, you will likely have greater diversity in terms of food, with dining selections ranging from Italian and Spanish to Middle Eastern and Asian cuisine. Some hotels provide buffet lunches and dinners. At certain resorts, you may choose an all-inclusive fee that includes meals and beverages. Regardless matter whether you pick all-inclusive or a la carte, eating in the Maldives is incredibly pricey. And if you're searching for a unique experience, try scheduling a seat at an underwater restaurant. Such alternatives include the Ithaa Undersea Restaurant in the Conrad Maldives Rangali Island Resort, 5.8 Undersea Restaurant at Hurawalhi Maldives, and Subsix at Niyama Private Islands Maldives.

MALDIVES VISA

A comprehensive guide on Getting a visa on arrival for the Maldives

The Maldives is a famous tourist destination for anybody wishing for a lavish holiday, surrounded by crystal blue seas and white sandy beaches. Considering how popular (and costly) a destination it is, the Maldives visa policy is relatively flexible.

Do I Need a Visa for Maldives?

No, you do not need a visa for the Maldives if you are visiting as a tourist. Nationals of all countries may receive a Maldives visa on arrival, free of charge, for stays of up to 30 days.

Also, Russian and Indian nationals may remain in the Maldives for up to 90 days without a visa.

How to Obtain a Maldives Visa on Arrival?
Everyone may receive a Maldives visa on arrival as long as they have the following papers to give to the Immigration officers:

- A machine-readable passport (MRP)/passport with Machine Readable Zone (MRZ), which is valid for at least another 6 months
- Pre-paid accommodation in the Maldives (e.g. a hotel reservation) (e.g. a hotel reservation)
- Evidence of adequate financial resources to support the full stay in the Maldives
- A return-flight ticket to your home nation or an onward-flight ticket
- A visa for your next destination (if necessary) (if required)

Note:

- You will not certainly acquire a Maldives visa on arrival for 30 days, since it is up to the Immigration authorities at the airport to determine for how long to allow you to enter.
- The Maldives visa on arrival is merely a tourist visa - you are not authorized to work in the Maldives with this visa under any conditions
- For any purposes other than tourism, you must have a sponsor in the Maldives to aid with the visa application.

Can You Extend a Maldives Visa on Arrival?

Yes, you may extend your Maldives visa on arrival by applying to the Maldives Immigration in Male before your existing visa expires. To apply, you have to submit a Visa Extension Application Form at the Immigration Head Office within official working hours. Immigration will evaluate whether you have the required financial resources to pay for the extended duration of your stay.

The maximum length of time you are permitted to remain in the Maldives is 90 days. Hence, if your current visa is 30 days, you may request a max 60-day extension.

The charge for an extension is Rufiyaa 750 if the total number of days you are spending (including those on the initial tourist visa) is more than 30. If even with the extension, you will be in the Maldives for fewer than 30 days, then you do not need to pay a charge.

Maldives Business Visa

- A Maldives business visa is provided online to foreign citizens going to the Maldives for their employment but without the purpose of being employed in a Maldivian firm. For the application, your sponsor (the firm you are visiting or a representative in the Maldives) needs to provide these papers through email to Maldives Immigration:
-
- Business Visa application form (form IM24) (form IM24)
- A scanned color copy of your passport's bio page. The passport must be machine-readable and valid for at least another six months.
- Your registration copy
- A recent passport-size picture of you

- Visa Applicant Information Form (IM30), if applicable
- A copy of your medical insurance coverage
- A letter from your sponsor, which indicates the date you want to remain in the Maldives
- Any additional supporting papers, such as your qualification certificates or a letter of experience
- All the papers have to be in PDF format. The photo must be in JPG format. You may get the relevant forms on the website of Maldives Immigration.

After you obtain online approval, you may go to the Maldives and collect your visa at the airport, by providing the original application papers specified above. You may seek a business visa at the Immigration Service at Velana International Airport or Gan International Airport.

How About Relocating to the Maldives?

If you want to truly relocate to the Maldives, then you will need a sponsor. Your sponsor needs to apply for your visa or residency permit with the Maldives Immigration in Male before you visit.

Supposing that you wish to relocate to the Maldives for work, then you will need to secure a position ahead so that your company may file for your work visa. The sponsor needs to be a local corporation in the Maldives or a locally-registered company.

Maldives Work Visa

For a Maldives work visa, your employer or agent in the Maldives needs to secure your work permit (Employment Authorization) from Maldives Immigration.

You and your sponsor have to provide the following documents:

- Your passport
- Copy of the Employment Approval
- Work Visa card charge, MVR50
- A current passport-size photo of you
- Medical health screening report produced by a medical institution approved by the appropriate government authority
- Work Visa submission receipt (IM29) (IM29)
- You may get the aforementioned paperwork and forms on the website of Maldives Immigration.

Working in the Maldives without a work permit is not permitted.

Maldives Marriage Visa

You need a Maldives marriage visa if you will marry a Maldivian native. Your sponsor (fiancée) needs to sponsor your visa before you fly by applying at the Maldives Immigration. You cannot get married or register your marriage in the Maldives if you hold an ordinary tourist visa. If you reach the country with your sponsored visa, then you may start the Marriage Visa process within 30 days.

The papers you require for a Maldives Marriage Visa are:

- Application for Permit Extension Form (IM23) (IM23). The application form must contain a signature and seal from the Family Court.

- Your passport. It must be a machine-readable passport.
- Original and copy of Marriage Certificate
- Copy of the Identification Card of the Maldivian national
- Passport-size photo of yourself
- Visa card charge, MVR50
- Proof of an expatriate health insurance policy
- Medical health screening report produced by a medical institution recognized by the appropriate government authority

You may obtain all the essential application forms on the website of Maldives Immigration.

Maldives Dependent Visa

If you are the dependant family member of a person already residing in the Maldives (such as a work visa holder), then your family member needs to sponsor your visa by providing the following documentation to Immigration:

- Application for Permit Extension From (IM23) (IM23)
- Your passport. It must be a machine-readable passport.
- Passport size photo of yourself
- Dependent Visa card cost, MVR50
- Dependent Visa cost, MVR750 for every 3 months
- A copy of the employment approval or visa card of the individual who has a Maldives work visa
- Evidence of family status (e.g. a marriage or birth certificate) (e.g. marriage or birth certificate)

- If you are the mother or father of the primary visa holder, you also need a letter from the appropriate embassy which outlines your living circumstances
- Copy of an expatriate health insurance policy
- Medical health screening report produced by a medical institution recognized by the appropriate government authority

You may get all the essential forms for the application on the website of Maldives Immigration.

DOS AND DON'TS IN THE MALDIVES

The Maldives is a lovely destination for anybody who enjoys the sun, beach, and seafood. Despite the resort islands being a universe of their own and having more permissive restrictions than the inhabited islands, the country itself is quite conservative.

If The Maldives is on your travel bucket list, check out these few things to keep in mind to avoid committing any faux pas and to guarantee you have a problem-free stay!

DON'TS
Be out late in Malé City
The capital city of the Maldives has a curfew that begins at about 10:00 pm. If you are waiting for a transfer to your island and have a little time to explore, make sure you're back inside in time to comply with

the requirement. For more things, you may not know about the Maldives.

Carry forbidden things on your vacation.

While visiting the Maldives, there are a few essential things to remember: A completely Muslim nation, the Maldives maintains a list of forbidden products that will not be permitted through customs. They include alcohol, any form of narcotics, pork, religious literature for distribution, and pets.

Participate in PDA in populated islands.

For heterosexual and Homosexual couples equally, public displays of love on non-resort islands such as Malé City are regarded as exceedingly disrespectful and may result in disciplinary action. This includes conduct that is accepted in the West, such as hand-holding and kissing.

Touch pink corals.

The local ecosystem is quite sensitive in the Maldives, so do your part to help life flourish! As you are snorkeling, take care not to harm any of the ecosystems around you. With that stated, The Maldives is one of the greatest destinations to dive in the world and is amazing when done eco-consciously.

Expect free or quick Wi-Fi.

Keep in mind that the Maldives is a distant chain of islands and won't have the same connection you may anticipate in a major metropolis. Several resorts do offer free Wi-Fi in their facilities but don't be shocked if the connection is poor and/or inconsistent. Just remember you're in paradise, so shut that device off and go explore the island instead!

Put off a vacation.

Being the world's lowest and flattest country, some of the islands are progressively vanishing. If the Maldives is on your travel bucket list, make 2023 the year it occurs. Don't miss a chance to experience these beautiful planets before they're gone forever!

DO
Dress modestly on populated islands.

A sensible rule of thumb in all conservative nations is to err on the side of caution. In inhabited islands, ladies should keep their shoulders and legs covered while males may choose to opt for long pants instead of shorts. Bikinis and topless sunbathing are legally forbidden outside of non-resort islands, but once you're at your resort, feel free to break out your holiday bikini!

Remove your shoes at the entrance of a house or mosque.

Before you enter a house or place of worship, remove your shoes. Mosques should be entered barefoot. If you're not sure whether you should remove your shoes, take a glance at what other people are doing and follow suit, or ask someone! The inhabitants are renowned for being extremely nice and accommodating to visitors, so don't be hesitant to check with someone if you're not sure what to do.

Be extremely considerate throughout Ramadan.

Having a 100% Muslim population, rigorous fasting is practiced by everyone throughout the month of Ramadan from dawn to sunset. Because of this, many eateries may be closed throughout the day. If you are on an inhabited island, avoid eating, drinking, or smoking in public.

Pick your keepsakes wisely.

Although things like crafts made from coral or turtle shells may be available for purchase on the islands, it is forbidden to export them. Make sure the souvenirs you chose are ones you can carry back with you!

Find out reef sites in the vicinity of your resort.

Depending on where you stay, you may be able to simply swim to the reefs, although certain resort islands are surrounded by lagoons and may need a boat journey to get to them. If being near the reef is crucial to you, inquire before you book to make sure your location is precisely what you want. Discover more of the greatest things to do in the Maldives.

Anticipate additional taxes owing to import prices.

In general, you will see a 10% service fee + 8% goods and services tax (which fluctuates regularly and may be greater by the time of your visit) on every receipt. Some resorts publish these on their public costs, like restaurant menus, while others do not. The taxes apply to anything you use or consume on the island including activities, rentals, spa services, meals, and beverages.

Bring plenty of sunblocks.

The island is on the equator, which means the sun's beams beat down at a 90-degree angle. The danger of sun damage rises there, so make sure to take plenty of sunscreens and sun protection such as hats, sleeves, and closely woven clothes.

MALDIVES 10 DAYS ITINERARY GUIDE

How to spend 10 days in Maldives –Option 1

If you want a stress-free holiday, consider this alternative, as it will be the appropriate one for you. This doesn't mean it will be restful, as you'll have plenty of things to fill your days, but you won't have such a hard time planning it, as it's mainly done for you already.

Start your journey with a 7 days island hopping tour. This tour covers all transport, tours, and lodging you need, and it even has part of the meals included (not all however so please check it out and see what you need to add) (not all though so please check it out and see what you need to add). You'll get to explore 3 native Maldives islands and do some water sports as well. This way, you get to know a little of the local culture, you get to experience some water sports, and you could even get to rest a bit on a beach if you like.

Upon return to Male (since the trip covers the journey back as well), you may continue your schedule with 3 days on a resort island. These are the islands that you see on postcards and PC backgrounds, but they're also less related to the Maldives essence, in my view.

When it comes to resorts, the sky is the limit. And your budget, of course. This will probably be the decisive factor when picking the resort you'll spend your days at. I have published a few blog pieces that could interest you, but let me offer you some suggestions here as well.

- – Bargain option: Reethi Beach resort – Check rates on Booking or Book on Agoda
- – Cheap water villas: Gangehi Island Resort & Spa – Check prices on Booking or Book on Agoda
- – Adults-only resort: Robinson Maldives – Check rates on Booking or Book on Agoda
- – Water villa with glass floor: Conrad Maldives Rangali Island Resort – Check rates on Booking or Book on Agoda
- - Water villa with jacuzzi: Adaaran Luxury Vadoo – Check rates on Booking or Book on Agoda

This is the easiest 10 days Maldives itinerary I managed to make for you. As you can see, it's not dull, but it takes minimum preparation from your side so you may rest as much as possible throughout your vacation, but won't be bored while doing so.

Things to do in 10 days in the Maldives-Option 2

This second method needs more preparation on your part, but with the correct tools that I'm offering here, you can schedule everything now and never worry about it until you get there. I have adjusted this in such a manner that your days will flow effortlessly, even though they'll be hectic occasionally.

Our itinerary begins with two days in Male, the capital city of the Maldives, and the location where you'll most certainly arrive. You will spend this time resting from the long journey you have undoubtedly had and learning a little about the culture of the location you're about to visit.

I have arranged days in Male at the beginning and conclusion of your vacation since you should stay near the airport on arrival and departure days. Your flight could always be delayed or your boat might have troubles while going back from an island, thus making your first and final night here a preferable alternative for lodging near the airport.

Where to stay in Male? So, try to choose a location that's near to the bikini beach, to be able to enjoy it when you have some free time. I recommend you don't spend much on accommodation here, since it's not worth that much on this island. Save your money for the resort and you won't regret it. Here are a few alternatives for you to pick from:

- – Small cheap option: Off Day Inn – Check costs on Booking or Book on Agoda
- – Mid-budget option: Marukab Plaza – Check rates on Booking or Book on Agoda
- – High budget option: Summer Beach – Browse rates on Booking or Book on Agoda

Day 1 – Enjoy a submarine trip from Male

Take this submarine tour and get to know the aquatic creatures you'll get to enjoy for the remainder of your vacation. This trip is especially fantastic for folks who don't do scuba diving since it's incredibly hard to appreciate what lies on the bottom of the ocean without really going there.

Day 2 – Take an eco-tour from Male

Since this place is protected for so many reasons, it's also highly vulnerable owing to so many severe external causes. Tourism is one of them, but also temperature changes that bleach the coral, humans who feed animals that interfere with the balance in the ecosystem, and god knows what else we're doing to this planet that we're not even aware of yet. Join an eco-tour from Male to discover more about conserving these pristine islands.

The second portion of the program will commence from the local island of Maafushi. This is a highly renowned island for budget tourists since it boasts some of the lowest alternatives for everything from hotels to excursions to eateries. This also makes it a touch too crowded for most people's liking, so bear this in mind while visiting.

I have picked this island for your next 3 days since you have enough things to attempt here. Don't get me wrong, you'll be able to do these things from the resort island as well, but it will cost you at least three times more, so maybe try to cover them here?

Additionally, I wanted you to sample a little of the local culture as well. We call this area paradise on earth, but for these individuals, it's simply home. It would be a pity for you to not visit this side of the Maldives as well, since this way you can enjoy the resort maybe even more. By the way, you may also get a day ticket to one of the resorts close-by, by if you can't wait to go there a few days later.

Where to stay in Maafushi? As I stated, the venue is fairly packed, so select the alternatives that match you best. Either save as much as possible by selecting a cheaper alternative or escape from the throng by renting a location closer to the bikini beach. Try out these ideas for inspiration:

- – Cheap option: Salt Beach Hotel – Check rates on Booking or Book on Agoda
- – Beach option: Kaani Palm Beach – Check rates on Booking or Book on Agoda
- – Deluxe option: Kaani Grand Seaview – Check rates on Booking or Book on Agoda

Day 3: Land on the island and begin fishing

The first day will be primarily spent on the boat on the trip here and set yourself up at the hotel. Spend your afternoon trying some local food at one of the eateries nearby, but don't eat too much since you'll go fishing in the evening. Enjoy this excursion and get to go fishing at sunset, then head to the BBQ meal that follows. What better way to conclude this busy day?

Day 4 – Go shipwreck snorkeling and encounter nurse sharks

Shipwrecks are not that numerous in the Maldives since the atmosphere is not the greatest for them, but you have this choice from Maafushi and you should make use of it. Get to observe the nurse sharks and marine life with this trip and be surprised at how nature has its way to recover.

Day 5 – Go snorkeling with manta rays

Mantas are among the greatest species you can see in the Maldives, so find a method to view them and be impressed by what this location has to offer. You will for sure be impressed by these gigantic, yet sweet creatures and you could even discover your new favorite activity to do in the Maldives.

Days 6-9 – Relax at a resort

The following four days of the program you'll spend on a resort island, soaking up the sun, resting as much as possible, drinking Mojitos, and having massages like there's no tomorrow. You may, of course, go paddle boarding or attempt any other water sports, or you can take yoga classes, go to the gym or even study something. However, I strongly suggest you simply relax on the beach and alternate between reading a nice book, enjoying the house reef and the crystal blue seas surrounding it, and napping in the sun (sunscreen is highly advised) (sunscreen is highly recommended).

Although you have kept your spending to a minimum until now, you can maybe afford to splurge a little on this section of your vacation. Attempt to include at least a massage while you're here, and if possible, acquire a fancier villa for at least a night. In the end, this is what the Maldives is renowned for so you may as well enjoy it.

When it comes to hotel possibilities, as I indicated, you can book anything from a few hundred dollars a night to a perfectly healthy kidney on the black market. Here are a few alternatives for a few pricing ranges, and try to remember the money-saving advice I mentioned at the beginning of the piece when scheduling your resort stay.

- – Small cheap option: Summer Island Maldives Resort – Check rates on Booking or Book on Agoda
- – Mid-budget option: Cocoon Maldives – Check rates on Booking or Book on Agoda
- – High budget option: The Nautilus Maldives – Check rates on Booking or Book on Agoda

TOP BEST HOTELS IN MALDIVES

To produce a detailed reference of the top hotels in the Maldives is no simple job. The archipelagic nation sets the benchmark when it comes to exceptional island life. It's where overwater stays come as usual, seclusion is a given and natural beauty is all about. The caliber is sky-high. Boutique stays and lo-fi boltholes are a rarity, instead, world-class hotels are spread out on their islands, nestling state-of-the-art spas and several restaurants between lush forests, immaculate beaches, and house reefs.

The current generation of Maldives hotels is taking this recipe one step further. It's not enough for only villas to be overwater anymore. Baths hangover lagoons now too, with glass flooring enabling customers to observe turtles as they get a massage. The typical pool bar has been trumped by a beachfront treehouse bar, and eateries have migrated underwater. Efforts towards sustainability are often widespread too. Most hotels have their conservation efforts and coral schemes. One is even solar-powered.

Which Maldives island is best?

When you hear The Maldives is made up of more than a thousand islands, the decision of 'which island?' may seem daunting. However, the option is really 'which hotel?'. The islands in the Maldives are small and often home to only one hotel, so a visit here is about experiencing one island paradise rather than bouncing about. If you're on a budget, you may want to choose a hotel that's a boat journey, rather than a seaplane flight, away from Malé, where the international airport lies. For additional recommendations, visit our inexpensive guide to the Maldives.

Which Maldives hotel is ideal for couples?

Being the stuff of honeymoon tales, the Maldives has lots to offer couples. For the genuinely remarkable destinations, we adore Cheval Blanc Randheli (as do the Duke and Duchess of Cambridge), and the Four Seasons Maldives at Landaa Giraavaru. Check our choice of the finest Maldives honeymoons for additional options.

Which Maldives hotel is ideal for families?

The Maldives may be best renowned for honeymoons, but its private island resorts are the stuff of family vacation fantasies too. Large villas ensure there's plenty of space for everyone, while kids' clubs, restaurants, and pools are all at your fingertips. Some of our top hotels for families are JW Marriott Maldives Resort and Spa and Fairmont

Maldives, Sirru Fen Fushi. For more, visit our guide to the top family hotels in the Maldives.

1. Kudadoo

If anybody knows what discerning tourists to the Maldives want, it's Lars Petre, the Swedish entrepreneur who not only founded the country's first sea-plane firm but co-manages nine additional island resorts. On Kudadoo, he has constructed the country's first solar-powered hotel and its first all-inclusive luxury hotel — all off a little coconut-forested sandbank.

Situated around a circular wooden walkway out to sea, its 15 rooms recall vast Japanese ryokans – created by New York-based architect Yuji Yamazaki from relaxing wood, stone, and reed-thatch, and fronted by a wide terrace, plunge pool, and stairway into the whirling blue water. When Petre says 'all-inclusive', he means it: whether that's two-hour Healing Earth treatments in the airy spa, a butler 24/7, jet-skiing and deep-sea fishing, or feasts involving fine wines (80 from Wine Spectator's Top 100 list) and impeccably presented dishes, from light Japanese teppanyaki to Maldivian seafood curry, concocted by French chef Antoine Lievaux, who has worked for Joël Robuchon and Alain Ducasse.

Surprisingly, because of the 989 solar panels that cover the open living room, there is not a single generator to be heard; only a quiet lap of waves on the beach, and the odd thud of a coconut. For more, check out our entire review of Kudadoo Island.

2. Emerald Faarufushi Resort & Spa

Searching for a Robinson Crusoe-style getaway? With powder-puff beaches and jungle green on the interior, with a blue lagoon packed with rainbow-colored parrotfish, blacktip reef sharks, and cow tail stingrays, this hotel is a spectacular addition to the Maldives. It's modest (only seven hectares) with 80 villas divided between overwater and beach.

There's no poor accommodation here; they all view that glittering, breath-stealing Indian Ocean, where ocean and sky mix flawlessly. You'll be allocated a personal butler, who'll schedule spa treatments, book you in for a game of tennis or excavate a heart-shaped seat for two in the sand. Food is a winner with five eateries to select from. Don't sleep on teriyaki chicken and locally-caught miso reef fish at Teppanyaki Grill.

Then there's the spellbindingly romantic overwater restaurant Mediterraneo, where you can feast on homemade tortellini and decadent tiramisu with stars overhead and lapping waves below, all washed down with as much house Champagne as you wish (this might be the smartest all-inclusive resort in the Maldives) (this might be the smartest all-inclusive resort in the Maldives).

Schedule up for a Balinese massage at the spa, tucked amid the trees with chattering terms for company. Snorkel, learn to dive, organize a wine tasting on a secluded sandbank, or just lounge on your villa's veranda and watch pods of dolphins plunging in the distance.

3. Gili Lankanfushi Maldives

When this place in the North Malé atoll came into life a little over 20 years ago (initially under sustainability hero Soneva's wing), Malé's international airport was nothing more than a tin hut, postcards were the major form of contact and most islands were without regular electricity.

The pancakes of sand encircling the capital were about as secluded a location as tourists could get to. Today, Gili Lankanfushi is regarded as within easy reach (just a 20-minute speedboat transfer), yachts and seaplanes crisscross the ocean and sky from morning until night and the nearby islands have street lights and a Coca-Cola factory. But relax, certain things never change.

This hotel is still positioned in one of the most eye-wateringly gorgeous lagoons in the nation, a picture of expansive white beaches, shape-shifting sandbanks, and seas that dance from peacock green to sapphire blue. All the houses here are perched above the ocean, keeping the island natural and the beaches on full brilliant display.

When a fire damaged the resort in 2019, it was a chance for regeneration. Interiors were refurbished, with hand-made wooden furniture and woven lampshades purchased from sustainable sources in Bali; bathrooms are filled with organic remedies and reef-safe sunscreen. For the ultimate Do Not Disturb vibe, maroon yourself in one of the clapboard Robinson Crusoe villas, cast out on the shores of the lagoon reachable by a short pontoon, where you can lay on your rooftop balcony tracing the spine of Scorpio across the night sky.

Putter back to the island and there's morning yoga; beach and jungle restaurants where food arrives fresh off the boat or gathered from organic gardens; and professional therapists from Thailand, Bali, and India at the Meera Spa.

Young coral being grown on ropes in the house reef will ultimately be transplanted in the sea in an attempt to develop reefs that are more resistant to climate-change bleaching (they also function as an underwater hammock for a giant green turtle that comes by most days) (they also work as an underwater hammock for a big green turtle that stops by most days).

Gili Lankanfushi has been working on its coral strategy for seven years — it was supporting sustainability long before it became a literal hot subject. And it's for that reason, as much as the lovely setting and great service, that it still stands head and shoulders above the pack.

4. Emerald Resort & Spa

A thrilling 45-minute seaplane trip from Malé, across deserted jungle islands and glittering blue lagoons, Emerald Resort and Spa seems like you're landed into your Bounty commercial. Situated on Fasmendhoo Island in Raa Atoll, with miles of infinite cotton-white beaches, excellent for snorkeling and diving, gin-clear seas with reef fish popping all around like confetti - manta rays, black-tip tiger sharks and dolphins - it's Finding Nemo on acid. There are 120 jaw-dropping houses here, divided between overwater and beach, created by American architect Edward

David Poole and constructed using bamboo, natural stone, and laughing leaves so they merge effortlessly with the tropical landscape. The style is simple and modern With contemporary furniture and plenty of sea-breezy hues. Overwater pool villas boast expansive marble bathrooms with deep bathtubs built for staring out over the ocean and the beach extending in both ways. The high life comes easy here with your own butler to take care of your every need - from ferrying you about in a buggy like a personal chauffeur to reserving tables and planning a private theater beneath the stars with handmade popcorn and beverages to boot, they're on it.

The hideaway provides a luxury all-inclusive package – and this could well be the smartest in the Maldives. There's Asiatique, where you'll feast on spectacular Asian grub (sticky wings, seafood gyoza), and Amazonica for mouth-tingling South American cuisine (red snapper ceviche in tiger's milk and Peruvian quinoa salads). Sprogs may run crazy without anybody batting an eyebrow owing to the biggest kids' club in the Maldives – great while you nest down at the Balinese-style spa. At dark, sit back on your deck and make a wish on a shooting star - there's not a trace of light pollution.

5. Joali

Famous Istanbul-based design company Autoban (behind London's Duck + Rice, the remarkable airport in Baku, and various hotels in their city such as the House Hotels and the Witt Suites) was commissioned to come up with something new and unusual at Joali. The decor features in the overwater and beach residences are carefully crafted. Locally hand-carved wood panels and bamboo-slatted headboards are counterbalanced with rose-gold bathroom taps like large stones. In the changing rooms, you'll discover heron-and-palm-leaf patterned kimonos by Ardmore and slippers like puffy clouds.

Joali is a combination of the finest that the Maldives has to offer. Show up barefoot at Mura Bar for a sunset Martini, a buttermilk-chicken slider, and a shisha pipe. Or get dolled up for supper at Japanese eatery Smoke.

It's this deep-rooted, robust luxury, without the least trace of prescribing who visitors should be, what they should dress, and how they should rest, that quickly connects Joali with the frontrunners. For Maldivophiles, here is a deserved winter-sun diversion that is every bit as high-achieving as some of the cherished old-timers and big-name brands.

6. Raffles Maldives Meradhoo

What could be more wonderful than a stay at Raffles? How about a stay at Raffles on the beach? So far south its skimming the equator – the delectable remoteness is well worth the lengthier transit time – this little island resort takes all the charm of its bigger Singapore brother and merges it with clotted-cream beaches, raspberry sunsets, and a coconut variant of its famed Sling. Free neck massages are doled out as you wait for breakfast (French boulangerie, Sri Lankan egg hoppers, detox drinks) with your feet on the sand.

Lunch may be the catch of the day – smoked tuna, perhaps, grilled with lemon oil. In the clever overwater spa, Balinese therapists give trademark massages that start with the hum of a Tibetan singing bowl and conclude with warm coconut oil being placed over your third eye. And the marine life is so abundant you can notice an aqua-menagerie without even getting your feet wet (20 hawksbill turtles have been documented as dwelling near the island) (20 hawksbill turtles have been recorded as living around the island).

7. Alila Kothaifaru Maldives

Joining an already overwhelming variety of luxury hotels strewn on white sand beaches in the turquoise-hued Indian Ocean, this latest addition holds it's own owing to top-notch service and a very 2020's clean-lined, austere style. Merely 80 villas, divided between over water (sunrise or sunset) and beach (properly veiled from one another by green foliage) are supported by two restaurants.

Sea Salt overlooking the sleek infinity pool and Ocean beyond where locally caught fish comes baked in sea salt or in a curry leaf bisque and Japanese-inspired Umami where melt-in-the-mouth Wagyu beef arrives in

Teriyaki style. There is a spa, with the treatment rooms raised on stilts to sit in the canopy line of the banyan and Indian almond trees, creating a relaxing, cocooning effect and there is a range of activities from coconut tastings to snorkeling amid lobsters and turtles on the house reef.

8. Jumeirah Maldives

A thrilling speedboat ride from the airport, on the fringes of the serene North Malé Atoll, is where Jumeirah has decided to make its comeback to the Maldives (having pulled out of the nation in late 2020). (having pulled out of the country in late 2020). The island of Olhuhali was formerly inhabited by Lux* North Malé and the Dubai-based hospitality group has stuck with the original's sleek South Beach Miami design while adding their own distinctly glitzy touch, from monogrammed bathrobes to new restaurants and live bands you really want to listen to. The 67 villas are among the biggest entry-level villas in the Maldives and are available in overwater and beach style. The former boast knee-trembling sunset vistas; the latter are more private; all have loads of outdoor space, enormous private pools, and spectacular rooftop decks for stargazing and outdoor movie evenings. Bathrooms are distinctly contemporary and concrete and contain tubs that drop down deep in the manner only hotel bathtubs ever do.

The sapphire-blue pool features flashes of red and an ice-cream cart right out of South Beach, while the Barium private dining area has aquariums for walls. And then, well, there is an Inti restaurant where the eye-roll-inducingly fresh ceviche blasts the regular menu of grilled fish out of these blue seas. The surrounding corals aren't in great health owing to climate change (something that's becoming more and more of a concern throughout the Maldives) but you can charter a jet ski in the morning and hang out with 100-strong pods of bottlenose dolphins catching breakfast just outside of the lagoon. Here is a location where the children of families who used to travel to the Maldives every year are now choosing to return to themselves as grown-ups.

9. Conrad Maldives

Having staked its claim on the beautiful all-natural twin islands of Rangali and Rangali Finolhu over a quarter of a century ago, Conrad's location remains one of the best of any resort in the Maldives – with long, broad stretches of sand wrapped around both jungly islands and manta rays pirouetting in the channel between. Yet there have been changes afoot: the installation of The Muraka (the world's first underwater hotel room) in 2018 was followed by a refurbishment of the cathedral-like beach villas in 2019, while the water villas had their turn this year. Fresh chef Christian Pedersen has infused new vitality into all 12 eateries. From the sand-between-your-toes breakfast to the healthful seared scallop and asparagus salads to the tasting menus at underwater restaurant Ithaa, his cuisine never fails to please. Opposition is useless but you can burn off any excesses by paddle-boarding around the lagoon marveling at sparkling parrotfish and sashaying reef sharks through a mesmeric azure lens.

10. JW Marriott Maldives Resort and Spa

There isn't a hibiscus out of place or a palm that hasn't been seen at this Indian Ocean replica of the white-picket beauty of the Hamptons. It's set in the far-northern Shaviyani atoll – where the neighboring islands are mostly undeveloped – so the seaplane transfer, at around an hour, takes a little longer than most, but the pay-off comes in the form of never-ending horizons, uninterrupted expanses of sea and crystal-clear night skies. It takes around 20 minutes to walk from one end of the island to the other, which makes it medium-sized by Maldivian standards.

Offshore there's a massive house reef – although the corals aren't in the greatest state (a sobering reminder of global warming) – but you can still see enormous white-tip reef sharks, moray eels, and clouds of shoaling fish. For larger marine thrills, the dolphin cruise provides sightings of hundreds rather than the normal handful in less distant regions or joins a fishing trip in pursuit of sailfish the size of kids. The Shaviyani atoll is a mega-fauna center. Back on dry ground, there are two large swimming pools, a glass-encased spa, a big kids' club, and 60 pool villas, designed like inverted galleons. Avoid the closely packed overwater type and opt for one on the beach instead, where each rests on its own big bougainvillea-veiled plot, only steps from the ocean, while the duplexes, with their upstairs dens, are perfect for families.

Inside, the décor strays from the usual Maldives teak-chic, embracing subtle tones of blue fabrics and amethyst-topped tables. Among the five great restaurants, lunchtime-only treetop Kaashi is a highlight for traditional Thai, and there are three bars: one near the Missoni-striped swimming pool and another selling 98 varieties of rum within a treehouse overlooking the beach. Although there aren't many surprises, this is an ultra-slick take on the tropical paradise template.

12 TOP BEACHES IN MALDIVES THAT YOU MUST VISIT

A network of 1,200 islands in the Indian Ocean, the Maldives is one of the calmest, most romantic, and most spectacularly picturesque locations in the world. The islands are packed into atolls, depending on their closeness to diverse coral reefs, and are surrounded by tranquil, azure-colored lagoons. These quiet waters give themselves to those lovely overwater bungalows that have become iconic with the island, while the coral reefs make it a sought-after snorkeling destination.

The third component of this exquisite holiday location is, of course, the Maldives beaches, many of which are immaculate, white-sand lengths that visitors spend lengthy days luxuriating on.

1. Cocoa Island

Cocoa Island, a magnificent getaway in the South Malé Atoll, is home to the exquisite COMO Cocoa Island resort. The island, also named Makunufushi, is noted for its sugar-sand beaches and crystal-clear seas. The living coral reefs — best experienced on a scuba diving expedition arranged by the COMO Cocoa Island crew — are one of the island's outstanding characteristics. The seclusion the beaches of Cocoa Island give to COMO visitors doesn't hurt either.

2. Landaa Giraavaru

Home to a Four Seasons resort, the picturesque coastlines of Landaa Giraavaru — one of the most desired private islands in the Maldives — are as exquisite as it gets. Visitors here will see a lengthy sandbank reaching into the turquoise lake that feels unearthly. The beaches that make up this paradisiacal island are, as the Four Seasons puts it, "a natural UNESCO Biosphere Reserve wilderness where iridescent blues, jungle greens, and dazzling whites meet innovation, conservation, and wellness with equal, dynamic intensity." To top it off, the ocean harbors manta rays, sea turtles, and a living reef demanding to be explored.

3. Baro's

The beaches of Baros island are immaculate, ringed by crystalline seas and a coral reef, which lends a fantasy dimension to the outstanding vistas. To explore the quiet Baros beaches, stay at the sole resort on this exclusive island: Baros Maldives. The hotel makes things extra memorable by permitting romantic candlelight meals on the smooth beach.

4. Reethi Rah

Some of the most remote beaches in the Maldives can be found on Reethi Rah – and only guests of One&Only Reethi Rah have access. Reethi Rah, nestled on three and a half miles of stunning shoreline, provides 12 exclusive and astoundingly gorgeous stretches of sand. It also has its time zone – an hour ahead of Malé — and as a consequence, offers some of the most spectacular sunsets in the Maldives. One&Only will put up loungers on the beach for families looking to spend the day in the sun, plus it provides villas with direct beach access.

5. Veligandu Island

Smooth sand, overwater villas, and a sandbar reaching as far as the eye can see - that's what awaits on Veligandu Island. The beach here is available solely to guests of the Veligandu Island Resort & Spa, an adults-only establishment in the North Ari

Atoll. Additionally, it's big enough that every hotel guest will feel as if they're on their stretch of beach. The beaches are also dotted with luxurious thatched-roof pavilions and loungers, and the reef encircling the island provides the ocean with infinite colors of green and blue.

6. Thulusdhoo Island

Capital of the Kaafu Atoll, Thulusdhoo is a Maldives surfing destination. Although many islands in the Maldives are populated by magnificent luxury hotels, there are a few local hot places, like Thulusdhoo, where tourists can experience the authentic culture of this magical archipelago. To reach Thulusdhoo, take an affordable, hour-and-a-half boat journey from Malé. There is a range of hotels to accommodate all budgets on the island. Visitors wishing to sunbathe can check out Tourist Beach, while experienced surfers chasing the greatest waves should go to Cokes Beach.

7. Hulhumale Island

Situated in the North Malé Atoll, Hulhumale is a man-made Maldives island. It provides a different vibe from many other islands in the archipelago – a more commercial and Westernized ambiance with lively hotels, shops, and restaurants. An atmosphere certainly worth experiencing for a weekend, Hulhumale's beaches are a joy, surrounded by coastal shops, restaurants, and water activity firms. Spend your day snorkeling, paddle boarding, or drinking a cocktail with your toes on the beach.

8. Fulhadhoo Island

Longer than it is broad, Fulhadhoo Island in the Baa Atoll is home to barely 250 inhabitants, peaceful, turquoise lagoons, and little natural ponds growing along the shore. A magnificent site to swim and dive in, Fulhadhoo harbors a plethora of fish species, dolphins, and turtles. Two hours from Malé by speedboat, it's also one of the quietest and most picturesque islands travelers may visit, with beaches that are mostly abandoned and an amazing possibility for animal encounters.

9. Ukulhas Island

Situated in the atoll Alif Alif Atoll, Ukulhas is an under-the-radar island having gorgeous beaches that are constantly cleaned to stimulate tourists and battle pollution. The island provides resorts in every price range, most only a short walk from the beach, albeit none with direct access to the sand. Yet, the beach is precisely why travelers flock to the island; it's an unbroken one-kilometer expanse of white sand, dotted with beach loungers and umbrellas. The beach is also calm and big enough that you'll never be without a lounge chair.

10. Omadhoo

Located inside the South Ari Atoll, Omandhoo is a tranquil island that has lately begun boosting its tourist options. The town, which makes up around 60 percent of the island, is home to 800 inhabitants. The island seems truly Maldives — Western habits are far less widespread here — and tourists interested in politely learning more about local culture will like the environment.

As for the beaches on Omadhoo, they are clean and calm, and tourists will adore the long sandbank going into the crystal-clear ocean. The reef around the beaches is home to schools of fish (including barracuda and snapper), turtles, and even whale sharks.

11. Dhigurah Island

In the South Ari Atoll, approximately 60 miles from the main island of Malé, sits Dhigurah Island. The island is noted for whale shark sightings, world-class diving, and beaches you'll never want to leave. Like Thulusdhoo, Dhigurah is home to various hotels and hot places for visitors and residents alike.

The gorgeous sandbar on Dhigurah has picnic tables, the island has its diving facility, and the water around the tiny sugar-sand beach is a meeting site for sea turtles and various types of colorful fish.

12. Hadahaa

Located in the North Huvadhoo Atoll, this island is home to the Park Hyatt Maldives Hadahaa and is encircled by a 360-degree house reef. The screensaver-worthy beaches, with natural white sand and appealing turquoise seas, are safeguarded by Park Hyatt's sustainability commitment to maintaining the reef healthy, the waterways and beaches clean, and reducing their total environmental effect.

To guarantee that these beaches remain some of the most spectacular in the Maldives, their development is monitored by Green Globe and a local marine scientist.

CONCLUSION

The Maldives is a tropical tourist resort in the Indian Ocean. The magnificent islands are quite peaceful and provide an experience that may best be characterized as a hideaway on a desert island but with high-quality accommodation, fantastic cuisine, superb service, and a large selection of activities.

The Maldives is easily accessible from Europe and Asia and many resorts have a very cosmopolitan environment whilst British visitors account for the largest number of guests after Italians, the islands are also very popular as a holiday destination for German, Japanese, Chinese, and Russian holidaymakers. Nevertheless, even if a resort is packed, it is typically still possible to locate a tranquil place with lots of private beaches.

The attraction of the Maldives as a honeymoon location is apparent, given the breathtaking environment and beautiful vistas. The location is also particularly child-friendly owing to the direct flights and resorts that provide well for families with kids' clubs and different activities as well as superb hotel alternatives. The blue sea around an island is generally rather shallow and excellent for youngsters to play in.

Printed in Great Britain
by Amazon